Table Of Contents

Introduction

Why Unity?

Why Unity?

Unity is a popular game engine that has become the go-to tool for many game developers, especially those interested in mobile game development. Here are some reasons why Unity is a great choice for creating mobile games:

1. Cross-platform development: Unity allows developers to create games for multiple platforms including iOS, Android, PC, and consoles. This means that you can create a game once and deploy it on multiple platforms, saving you time and money in the long run.

2. Easy to use: Unity has a user-friendly interface and is easy to learn, even for beginners. The drag-and-drop functionality and visual scripting tools make it easy to create game objects, add components, and create interactions.

3. Large community: Unity has a large and active community of developers who share tips, tricks, and tutorials online. This means that if you ever get stuck, there are plenty of resources available to help you out.

4. Asset store: Unity has an asset store where developers can buy and sell assets such as game objects, scripts, and plugins. This makes it easy to find and use assets that can speed up your game development process.

5. Performance: Unity is known for its high performance, which is important for mobile game development. It can handle complex graphics and physics calculations, while still maintaining a smooth frame rate.

Overall, Unity is a great choice for anyone interested in mobile game development. Its cross-platform capabilities, ease of use, large community, asset store, and performance make it a top choice for game developers of all skill levels.

Who is this book for?

Who is this book for?

Are you an aspiring game developer looking to create fun and engaging games for mobile devices? Do you have no prior experience in game development, but are eager to learn the ropes? If so, then Unity Game Development for Beginners is the book for you!

This book is specifically designed for anyone who wants to create games, particularly those interested in mobile game development with Unity. Even if you have never written a line of code before, this step-by-step guide will take you through the process of creating your first game, from setting up your development environment to publishing your finished product.

Whether you are a student, hobbyist, or aspiring game developer, this book is perfect for beginners who are looking for a comprehensive introduction to game development with Unity. It is also ideal for those who have dabbled in game development in the past but have not yet mastered the tools and techniques needed to create a successful mobile game.

The book is written in a clear and concise language, making it easy to understand even the most complex concepts. It covers all the essential elements of mobile game development, including game design, graphics, sound, and user interface. You will learn how to create and animate game objects, design levels and environments, and develop game mechanics and AI.

The book also includes real-world examples and practical exercises that will help you apply what you learn to your own game projects. By the end of the book, you will have the skills and knowledge necessary to create your own mobile games and publish them on popular app stores.

In summary, Unity Game Development for Beginners is the perfect resource for anyone who wants to get started in game development. It is a comprehensive guide that will teach you everything you need to know to create mobile games using Unity. Whether you are a complete beginner or an experienced developer looking to expand your skills, this book has something to offer. So, what are you waiting for? Start your game development journey today!

What will you learn?

In this subchapter, we will be discussing what you can expect to learn from reading Unity Game Development for Beginners: A Step-by-Step Guide to Creating Mobile Games. Whether you are a complete beginner or have some experience with game development, this book is designed to help you get started with mobile game development using Unity.

First and foremost, you will learn the basics of Unity and how to use it to create mobile games. We will cover everything from installing Unity to creating your first game scene. You will learn how to use the Unity editor, import assets, and create basic game mechanics.

Next, we will dive deeper into game development and cover topics such as game physics, animation, and sound effects. You will learn how to create realistic game environments, add special effects, and create immersive soundscapes.

As we progress, we will explore different game genres and create games such as platformers, puzzle games, and endless runners. You will learn how to create game mechanics specific to each genre and how to design levels that challenge players.

In addition to game development, you will also learn about game publishing and marketing. We will cover topics such as app store optimization, social media marketing, and monetization strategies. You will learn how to publish your game to the app stores and how to promote it to reach a wider audience.

Finally, we will wrap up by discussing advanced topics such as multiplayer game development, virtual reality, and augmented reality. You will learn how to create multiplayer games that can be played online, as well as how to create immersive virtual and augmented reality experiences.

In conclusion, Unity Game Development for Beginners: A Step-by-Step Guide to Creating Mobile Games is a comprehensive guide that covers everything you need to know to get started with mobile game development using Unity. Whether you are a complete beginner or have some experience with game development, this book will help you take your skills to the next level and create amazing mobile games.

Setting Up Unity

Installing Unity

Installing Unity

Before you can start creating mobile games with Unity, you need to install the software on your computer. Unity is available for both Windows and Mac operating systems, and you can download it for free from the Unity website.

Once you've downloaded the installer, double-click it to begin the installation process. You'll be asked to accept the license agreement and choose a destination folder for the installation. You can also choose to install additional components, such as the Unity Hub and Visual Studio, which can be useful for managing your projects and writing code.

Once the installation is complete, you can launch Unity and begin creating your first project. Unity provides several project templates to help you get started, including 2D and 3D game templates, as well as templates for augmented reality (AR) and virtual reality (VR) applications.

If you're new to Unity, it's a good idea to start with one of the basic game templates and work your way up from there. The basic game templates provide a simple game environment and basic player controls, so you can focus on learning the Unity interface and mechanics.

As you become more comfortable with Unity, you can start customizing your projects and adding more advanced features, such as physics simulations, AI-controlled characters, and multiplayer networking.

Overall, installing Unity is a straightforward process that shouldn't take more than a few minutes. Once you have the software installed, you'll have access to a powerful game development platform that can help you create mobile games that are fun, engaging, and profitable. So don't hesitate to take the plunge and start your journey into mobile game development with Unity today!

Understanding the Unity interface

Understanding the Unity interface is crucial for anyone who wants to create mobile games using Unity. Unity is a powerful game engine that allows game developers to create amazing games with ease. The Unity interface is designed to make game development easy and intuitive, but it can be overwhelming for beginners. In this chapter, we will take a closer look at the Unity interface and explain its various components.

The Unity interface consists of several windows and panels. The most important of these are the Scene view, Game view, Hierarchy window, Inspector window, and Project window. The Scene view is where you design your game environment, while the Game view is where you play your game. The Hierarchy window is where you manage the objects in your game, while the Inspector window is where you modify the properties of those objects. The Project window is where you organize your game assets.

In addition to these windows and panels, Unity also has a toolbar that contains various tools for game development. The toolbar includes tools for manipulating objects, creating new objects, and navigating the scene.

One of the key features of Unity is its drag-and-drop functionality. You can drag and drop assets and objects from the Project window into the Scene view to create your game environment. You can also drag and drop scripts onto objects to add functionality to your game.

Another important aspect of the Unity interface is the use of prefabs. Prefabs are reusable objects that you can create and modify in the Project window. You can then drag and drop these prefabs into the Scene view to create new instances of the object.

Overall, understanding the Unity interface is essential for mobile game development with Unity. Once you are familiar with the Unity interface, you can start creating your own games with ease. With the help of this chapter, you will be able to navigate the Unity interface and create your own game environments in no time.

Creating your first Unity project

Creating your first Unity project is an exciting step towards achieving your goal of becoming a mobile game developer. In this chapter, we will guide you through the process of creating your first Unity project, and by the end of it, you will have a basic understanding of the Unity interface and how to create a simple game.

Firstly, you need to download and install the latest version of Unity from the official website. Once you have installed Unity, open the software and create a new project by clicking on the "New" button. Give your project a name and select the location where you want to save it. It is important to keep your project organized by creating folders for different assets and scripts.

Next, you will be taken to the Unity interface, which can be overwhelming for beginners. The interface consists of multiple windows, including the Scene view, Game view, Hierarchy, Inspector, and Project. Take some time to familiarize yourself with these windows and their functions.

To create a simple game, you need to create a scene. A scene is where you will design your game environment and place objects such as characters and obstacles. To create a scene, click on "File" and select "New Scene." You will be taken to the Scene view, where you can start designing your game environment by adding objects from the Project window.

In Unity, objects are referred to as GameObjects. To add a GameObject to your scene, click on "GameObject" in the menu bar and select the type of object you want to add. For example, you can add a Cube or a Sphere. Once you have added an object, you can modify its properties in the Inspector window, such as its position, rotation, and scale.

To test your game, you need to add a camera to your scene. The camera will act as the player's perspective and enable them to see the game environment. To add a camera, click on "GameObject" and select "Camera." You can modify the camera's properties in the Inspector window, such as its position and field of view.

Congratulations, you have created your first Unity project! Although this is just the beginning, you have taken the first step towards becoming a mobile game developer. In the next chapter, we will cover how to add functionality to your game by scripting in C#.

Understanding Game Objects

What are game objects?

Game objects are the building blocks of any game development project in Unity. They are the fundamental elements that make up the game world and interact with each other to create the game experience. Understanding game objects is crucial for anyone who wants to create games, especially beginners in mobile game development with Unity.

In Unity, a game object is any object that can be placed in the game world. It can be anything from a character, a building, a weapon, or even a sound effect. Each game object has its own set of properties, such as position, rotation, scale, and components. Components are the scripts, meshes, textures, and other assets that make up the game object and dictate its behavior.

Game objects can interact with each other through components. For example, a player character may have a component that allows it to move, jump, and shoot. A weapon game object may have a component that allows it to fire projectiles. When the player character comes into contact with the weapon, the weapon's component can trigger a response, such as firing a projectile at the player character.

In Unity, game objects can also be organized into hierarchies. A hierarchy is a way of grouping game objects together and creating a parent-child relationship between them. This allows for easier management and manipulation of multiple game objects at once. For example, a building game object may have child game objects for its walls, windows, and doors. By selecting the parent game object, all of its child game objects can be selected and manipulated at once.

Game objects can also have prefabs. A prefab is a pre-made game object that can be saved and reused throughout a project. This saves time and effort by allowing developers to create one game object and use it multiple times in different parts of the game world.

In conclusion, game objects are the building blocks of any game development project in Unity. They are the fundamental elements that make up the game world and interact with each other to create the game experience. Understanding game objects is crucial for anyone who wants to create games, especially beginners in mobile game development with Unity. By mastering game objects, developers can create complex and engaging games with ease.

Creating game objects

Creating game objects is one of the primary tasks a game developer needs to master when creating mobile games using Unity. Game objects are the building blocks of a game, and they can represent anything from characters, obstacles, items, to background elements.

To create a new game object in Unity, you can go to the Hierarchy window and click on the "Create" button. From there, you can select the type of game object you want to create, such as a cube, sphere, or capsule. You can also create more complex game objects by combining different shapes and components.

Once you have created a game object, you can customize it by adding components to it. Components are scripts that define the behavior and properties of a game object. For example, you can add a "Rigidbody" component to make a game object move and respond to physics, or you can add a "Mesh Renderer" component to make it visible.

To add a component to a game object, you can either click on the "Add Component" button in the Inspector window or drag-and-drop the component from the Assets window onto the game object. You can also customize the properties of a component by changing its values in the Inspector window.

Another important aspect of creating game objects is organizing them into a hierarchy. The Hierarchy window allows you to arrange game objects in a parent-child relationship, where the parent object acts as a container for its child objects. This can be useful for keeping your game objects organized and for controlling their behaviors and properties.

In conclusion, creating game objects is a fundamental skill that every mobile game developer using Unity needs to master. By understanding how to create, customize, and organize game objects, you can create engaging and immersive games that captivate your audience.

Transforming game objects

Transforming Game Objects

In Unity, game objects are the building blocks of any game. They can be anything from characters and enemies to power-ups and collectibles. However, simply creating game objects is not enough. You need to be able to transform them in order to give them life and make them interact with the game world.

Transforming game objects in Unity is a simple process. There are three main components that you need to be familiar with: position, rotation, and scale.

Position

The position of a game object is its location in the game world. You can change the position of a game object by adjusting its X, Y, and Z coordinates. For example, if you want to move a character to the left, you would decrease its X coordinate. If you want to move it up, you would increase its Y coordinate.

Rotation

The rotation of a game object is its orientation in the game world. You can rotate a game object around its X, Y, and Z axes. For example, if you want to rotate a character to the left, you would rotate it around its Y axis.

Scale

The scale of a game object is its size in the game world. You can increase or decrease the scale of a game object by adjusting its X, Y, and Z values. For example, if you want to make a character bigger, you would increase its X, Y, and Z values.

Transforming game objects is essential for creating dynamic and interactive games. It allows you to move, rotate, and scale game objects in order to create unique gameplay experiences. With Unity, transforming game objects is a breeze. You simply need to select the game object you want to transform and adjust its position, rotation, and scale values.

In conclusion, transforming game objects is a fundamental skill that every mobile game developer using Unity should master. With the ability to transform game objects, you can create engaging and interactive gameplay experiences that keep players coming back for more. So, start experimenting with transforming game objects today and see how it can enhance your mobile game development with Unity.

Understanding the hierarchy

Understanding the Hierarchy

In Unity game development, the hierarchy is an essential tool that allows you to organize and manage the different elements of your game. It is a tree-like structure that represents the parent-child relationships between game objects.

A game object is any element that can be placed in the game world, such as characters, scenery, or props. Each game object has a set of components that define its behavior, appearance, and interaction with other objects. Examples of components include rigid bodies, colliders, scripts, and audio sources.

To create a hierarchy, you can simply drag and drop game objects onto each other in the Scene view or the Hierarchy window. The parent-child relationship means that any changes made to a parent object will affect all its child objects. For example, if you move a parent object, all its children will move with it.

The hierarchy also determines the order in which objects are rendered on the screen. Objects higher up in the hierarchy are rendered first, meaning that they will appear in front of objects lower down in the hierarchy. This is important to keep in mind when creating complex scenes with overlapping objects.

Another important aspect of the hierarchy is the concept of prefabs. A prefab is a template of a game object that can be reused multiple times in your game. By creating a prefab, you can make changes to the template, and those changes will be applied to all instances of that prefab in your game. This is a powerful feature that can save you a lot of time and effort when designing your game.

Understanding the hierarchy is essential for mobile game development with Unity. As you create more complex games, you will need to manage a large number of game objects and components. The hierarchy is a powerful tool that can help you organize and manage your game elements efficiently. By mastering the hierarchy, you will be able to create games that are both visually appealing and easy to manage.

Using Components

What are components?

Components are the building blocks of any Unity game. They are the individual pieces that make up a game object, and they define the object's behavior and appearance.

Every game object in Unity is made up of one or more components. These components can be added, removed, and modified to change the way an object behaves. For example, if you want a game object to move, you can add a Rigidbody component to it. If you want it to display an image, you can add a Sprite Renderer component.

Components can be found in the Unity Editor's Component menu. There are many different types of components, each with its own unique functionality. Some of the most commonly used components include:

- Transform: This component defines the position, rotation, and scale of a game object in 3D space.

- Rigidbody: This component adds physics to a game object, allowing it to move and interact with other objects in a realistic way.

- Collider: This component defines the shape of a game object and allows it to detect collisions with other objects.

- Renderer: This component is responsible for rendering a game object's appearance, such as its texture or material.

Components can also be created and customized using scripts. This allows you to create custom behaviors and functionality for your game objects.

One of the benefits of using components in Unity is that they can be reused and shared between different game objects. This can save time and make your game development process more efficient.

In conclusion, components are a vital part of Unity game development. They allow you to define the behavior and appearance of your game objects, and they can be customized and shared to make your development process more efficient. By understanding how components work, you can create more complex and interactive games with ease.

Adding and removing components

Adding and removing components is an essential skill for any game developer working with Unity. Components are the building blocks of your game, and they control everything from physics and movement to sound and visual effects. In this section, we'll show you how to add and remove components in Unity, so you can create the game of your dreams.

Adding Components

Adding components to game objects in Unity is a simple process. First, select the game object you want to add a component to. Then, click the Add Component button in the Inspector panel. This will open a drop-down menu with all the available components in Unity.

To add a component, simply click on the component you want to add. For example, if you want to add a Rigidbody component to your game object, click on Rigidbody in the drop-down menu. Once you've added the component, you can customize its properties in the Inspector panel.

Removing Components

Removing components is just as easy as adding them. To remove a component, select the game object that has the component you want to remove. Then, click on the component in the Inspector panel to select it. Finally, click the Remove Component button to remove the component from the game object.

It's important to note that removing a component will also remove any settings or functionality associated with that component. So, make sure you're certain you want to remove a component before doing so.

Conclusion

In conclusion, adding and removing components is a basic but essential skill for any game developer working with Unity. These simple actions can greatly impact the functionality and design of your game. Remember, always be sure you want to remove a component before doing so, and experiment with adding different components to see how they affect your game. With these tools at your disposal, you'll be well on your way to creating the mobile game of your dreams.

The most commonly used components

When it comes to game development with Unity, there are a number of components that are commonly used. These components form the building blocks for creating games and are essential for any beginner looking to get started in game development. In this section, we will explore some of the most commonly used components in Unity and how they are used in game development.

1. GameObjects: GameObjects are the basic building blocks of any Unity scene. They are the objects that you place in your game world and can include things like characters, obstacles, and items. Each GameObject can have its own set of components and properties that define its behavior and appearance.

2. Transform: The Transform component is used to define the position, rotation, and scale of a GameObject. It allows you to move, rotate, and resize objects in your game world.

3. Collider: Colliders are used to detect collisions between GameObjects. They can be used to create physical barriers or to trigger events when two objects collide.

4. Rigidbody: The Rigidbody component is used to add physics to a GameObject. It can be used to simulate gravity, apply forces, and create realistic movement for objects in your game world.

5. Scripting: Scripting is used to add custom behavior to your GameObjects. You can write scripts in C# or UnityScript to control the behavior of your objects, create game logic, and handle user input.

6. Animation: The Animation component is used to create animated sequences for your GameObjects. You can create animations for things like character movements, object interactions, and special effects.

7. Audio: The Audio component is used to add sound effects and music to your game. You can import audio files and use the Audio component to control playback and volume.

In conclusion, these are just a few of the most commonly used components in Unity game development. As a beginner, it is important to become familiar with these building blocks in order to create engaging and interactive games. With practice and experimentation, you can combine these components to create unique and exciting game experiences.

Scripting in Unity

What is scripting?

What is scripting?

Scripting is a term commonly used in game development, and it refers to the process of writing code that controls the behavior of game objects. In Unity game development, scripting is done using the C# programming language.

Scripts are an essential part of game development because they enable developers to create interactive and dynamic games. With scripts, you can give game objects behavior, such as movement, animation, and interaction with other game elements. Scripts can also be used to create game logic, such as scoring systems, game rules, and AI behavior.

One of the advantages of Unity game development is that it provides a visual scripting system called Unity Editor. Unity Editor allows you to create scripts without having to write code manually. Instead, you can use a drag-and-drop interface to create behaviors and game logic using pre-built components.

However, it is important to note that visual scripting systems have their limitations. They may not offer the same level of control and flexibility as writing code manually. Therefore, it is essential to learn how to write code in C# to become a proficient Unity game developer.

If you are new to game development, learning how to write scripts might seem overwhelming at first. However, with practice and patience, you can master the basics of scripting and create your own games.

To get started with scripting in Unity, it is recommended that you learn the basics of C# programming. There are many resources available online that can help you learn C#, such as tutorials, videos, and online courses.

Once you have learned the basics of C#, you can start creating scripts using Unity Editor. The Unity website provides comprehensive documentation on how to write scripts using Unity Editor. Additionally, there are many online communities where you can ask for help and share your projects with other Unity game developers.

In conclusion, scripting is an essential aspect of Unity game development. It enables developers to create interactive and dynamic games that engage players. Whether you are a beginner or an experienced game developer, learning how to write scripts in Unity is a crucial step in creating your own mobile games.

Creating scripts in Unity

Creating scripts in Unity is an essential aspect of mobile game development. Scripts are the building blocks of any game, and they enable you to add functionality to game objects, create interactive elements, and control game mechanics. To create a successful mobile game, you need to have a solid understanding of how to write scripts in Unity.

The first step in creating scripts is to understand the Unity scripting language. Unity uses C# (pronounced C sharp) as its scripting language, which is a popular and powerful language used by many developers. C# is easy to learn, and it is a great language for beginners to start with. If you are new to programming, it is recommended that you start with the basics of C# before diving into Unity scripting.

Once you have a basic understanding of C#, you can start creating scripts in Unity. Unity has a powerful and intuitive scripting interface, which makes it easy to create scripts. You can create new scripts by selecting the appropriate menu option or by using the shortcut keys.

When creating a script, you need to define the variables, functions, and classes that will be used in your game. Variables are used to store data, functions are used to perform tasks, and classes are used to define objects. You can also use pre-existing scripts from the Unity Asset Store or other sources to speed up your development process.

Another important aspect of creating scripts in Unity is debugging. Debugging is the process of finding and fixing errors in your code. Unity has a built-in debugger that allows you to step through your code and identify errors. You can also use third-party debugging tools to make the process easier.

In conclusion, creating scripts in Unity is an essential part of mobile game development. By understanding the Unity scripting language, defining variables, functions, and classes, and debugging your code, you can create engaging and interactive mobile games. With practice and perseverance, you can become an expert in Unity scripting and create amazing mobile games that people will love to play.

Understanding C# basics

C# is a powerful and popular programming language that is widely used in mobile game development with Unity. Understanding the basics of C# is essential for anyone who wants to create games, especially beginners. In this subchapter, we will cover the fundamental concepts of C# that you need to know to get started with Unity game development.

Variables and Data Types

Variables are used to store data in a program. In C#, there are several data types that you can use to define variables, such as int, float, string, bool, and more. Understanding the data types and how to declare and use variables is crucial for writing C# code.

Control Structures

Control structures are used to control the flow of a program. In C#, there are three types of control structures: loops, if-else statements, and switch statements. These structures allow you to perform different actions based on conditions, iterate over a set of data, or break out of a loop.

Functions and Methods

Functions and methods are used to perform specific tasks in a program. In C#, you can define your own functions and methods or use the built-in ones. Understanding how to declare and call functions and methods is essential for writing C# code.

Classes and Objects

Classes and objects are the building blocks of object-oriented programming. In C#, a class is a blueprint for creating objects, and an object is an instance of a class. Understanding how to create and use classes and objects is crucial for developing complex games.

Conclusion

Understanding C# basics is essential for anyone who wants to create mobile games with Unity. This subchapter covered some of the fundamental concepts of C# that you need to know to get started with Unity game development, such as variables and data types, control structures, functions and methods, and classes and objects. With this knowledge, you can start writing C# code and build amazing games.

Controlling game objects with scripts

Controlling game objects with scripts is a fundamental aspect of game development. With Unity, you can use scripts to create complex behaviors and interactions between game objects, allowing you to create engaging and exciting games for mobile devices.

In Unity, scripts are written using the C# programming language. C# is a powerful language that allows you to create complex scripts that can control every aspect of your game objects. With C#, you can control movement, animations, physics, and much more.

To create a script in Unity, you first need to create a new script file in your project. You can do this by selecting "Create" from the Project window, then selecting "C# Script". Once you have created your script file, you can open it in your preferred code editor and start writing your code.

One of the most common uses of scripts in Unity is to control the movement of game objects. You can use scripts to define the speed and direction of movement, as well as to detect collisions and other interactions with other game objects.

For example, you might create a script that controls the movement of a character in your game. This script could define the character's speed and direction, as well as handle input from the player to control the character's movement.

Another common use of scripts in Unity is to control animations. You can use scripts to trigger animations based on specific events, such as when a player completes a level or collects a power-up.

Overall, controlling game objects with scripts is a powerful tool for mobile game development with Unity. By using scripts, you can create complex interactions and behaviors that make your games more engaging and exciting for players. Whether you are a beginner or an experienced game developer, learning how to use scripts in Unity is an essential skill for creating mobile games.

Creating Scenes

What are scenes?

Scenes are an essential component of Unity game development, especially when it comes to creating mobile games. A scene is a self-contained environment within Unity, where you can add and manipulate game objects, camera angles, and lighting settings. It is like a canvas where you can build your game world, design levels, and create different game states.

In Unity, you can create multiple scenes, each with its unique set of game objects and settings. For example, you can have a scene for the main menu, another for the game level, and one for the end credits. Each scene can have its own camera, lighting, and audio settings, enabling you to create a seamless transition between different game states.

Scenes are essential for creating mobile games because they help optimize the game's performance. By breaking down the game into multiple scenes, you can load only the necessary assets and game objects, reducing the game's memory usage and increasing its performance. This is particularly important for mobile games, where device resources are limited, and performance is critical.

To create a new scene in Unity, you can select "File > New Scene" from the menu bar. You can then add game objects to the scene, adjust their position and rotation, and customize their properties using the Inspector window. You can also add cameras, audio sources, and lighting to the scene to create different moods and atmospheres.

Once you have created multiple scenes, you can link them together using Unity's SceneManager API. For example, when the player clicks on the "Start Game" button in the main menu, you can load the game level scene, and when the player completes the level, you can load the end credits scene. This creates a seamless transition between different game states, enhancing the player's experience.

In conclusion, scenes are a crucial aspect of Unity game development, especially for mobile games. By creating multiple scenes and optimizing their performance, you can create engaging and immersive game experiences for your players.

Creating scenes in Unity

Creating scenes in Unity is an essential part of game development. A scene is a level or area in your game where the player can interact with the environment and characters. Creating scenes in Unity is easy and straightforward, and it allows you to design and build your game world, add characters, and make them interact with each other.

The first step in creating a scene in Unity is to open the Unity editor and create a new project. Once you have created a new project, you can start building your game world. To create a new scene, click on File > New Scene in the top-left corner of the editor. This will open a new empty scene where you can start building your game.

To add objects to your scene, click on the GameObject menu at the top of the editor and select the type of object you want to add to your scene. You can add a camera, a player character, enemies, and any other elements that you want to include in your game world. Once you have added your objects, you can position and scale them to fit your scene.

To create a terrain in your scene, you can use Unity's built-in Terrain tool. This tool allows you to create hills, mountains, and other terrain features by sculpting the terrain using different brushes. You can also add textures and vegetation to your terrain to make it look more realistic.

Once you have created your scene and added all the necessary elements, you can start scripting the behavior of your characters and objects. Unity uses C# as its scripting language, and you can use it to create custom behaviors for your characters and objects. You can also add sound effects and music to your game using Unity's audio system.

In conclusion, creating scenes in Unity is an essential part of game development. It allows you to design and build your game world, add characters and objects, and make them interact with each other. With Unity's intuitive editor and powerful scripting system, creating scenes for your mobile game has never been easier.

Adding game objects to scenes

Adding game objects to scenes is one of the fundamental building blocks of game development using Unity. Game objects are the basic units of all games, and they represent the different elements that make up the game world. In this subchapter, we will discuss how to add game objects to scenes and how to manipulate them to create engaging gameplay experiences.

To add a game object to a scene, you need to select the "GameObject" menu from the top menu bar in Unity. This will open up a drop-down menu that provides you with a list of different types of game objects that you can add to your scene. Some of the most commonly used game objects include cubes, spheres, and planes. You can also add more complex objects such as characters, props, and vehicles.

Once you have selected the game object you want to add to your scene, you can simply drag it from the hierarchy window and drop it into the scene view. You can then use the transform tools to manipulate the object's position, rotation, and scale. This will allow you to position the object precisely where you want it in the scene.

To create a more complex game object, you can use Unity's prefab system. A prefab is a pre-made object that you can use repeatedly in your game. To create a prefab, you simply select the game object you want to use as a template, and then drag it into the project window. This will create a new prefab asset that you can use in your game.

In addition to adding game objects to scenes, you can also use Unity's scripting system to add behavior to your game objects. This will allow you to create more complex gameplay mechanics and interactions between different objects in your game.

In conclusion, adding game objects to scenes is a fundamental aspect of game development using Unity. By understanding how to add and manipulate game objects, you can create engaging and immersive gameplay experiences for your players. Whether you are a beginner or an experienced game developer, mastering this skill is essential for creating successful mobile games with Unity.

Switching between scenes

Switching between scenes is a crucial aspect of game development. It allows developers to create a seamless gaming experience by navigating between different levels, menus, and game modes. In this subchapter, we will discuss how to switch between scenes using Unity, a popular game development engine.

The first step in switching between scenes is to create the scenes themselves. In Unity, a scene is simply a level or game mode that players can navigate to. To create a new scene, go to File > New Scene, or press Ctrl + N. You can then add objects, characters, and other elements to the scene using Unity's user-friendly interface.

Once you have created your scenes, it's time to start switching between them. One of the most common ways to switch between scenes is to use a button or trigger in one scene that loads another scene when clicked. To do this, you will need to use Unity's SceneManager class, which allows you to manage and switch between scenes.

To create a button that loads a new scene, first, create a new script in Unity by right-clicking in the Project panel and selecting Create > C# Script. Then, attach the script to the button object by dragging it onto the object in the Scene view. In the script, you will need to use the SceneManager.LoadScene method to load the new scene when the button is clicked.

Another way to switch between scenes is to use Unity's built-in scene management tools, such as the Scene Manager window. This window allows you to view and manage all of your scenes in one place, making it easy to switch between them during development.

In addition to these methods, Unity also supports more advanced scene switching techniques, such as asynchronous loading and additive scenes. These techniques can help you create more complex and dynamic game experiences, but may require more advanced knowledge of Unity and game development in general.

In conclusion, switching between scenes is an essential skill for any mobile game developer using Unity. By understanding how to create and switch between scenes, you can create a more immersive and engaging gaming experience for your players. With Unity's powerful tools and resources, there's no limit to what you can create.

User Interface

What is the user interface?

The user interface (UI) is a crucial aspect of any game, including mobile games developed with Unity. It refers to the various visual and interactive elements that allow players to navigate the game, interact with objects and characters, and access game settings and information.

In mobile games, the UI is particularly important because players interact with the game using touchscreens, which require intuitive and responsive UI design. Unity provides a range of tools to create UI elements, such as buttons, sliders, text fields, and images. These elements can be arranged in various layouts and hierarchies to create complex UI systems.

One of the key concepts in UI design is usability, which refers to how easy and intuitive the UI is for players to use. A usable UI should be visually appealing, easy to navigate, and provide clear feedback to players when they interact with it. This can be achieved through careful consideration of factors such as color, typography, layout, and animation.

Another important aspect of UI design is accessibility, which refers to how well the UI accommodates players with different abilities and preferences. This includes considerations such as font size, color contrast, and support for different input methods such as keyboard and gamepad.

In Unity, UI elements can be created and edited using the Unity UI system, which provides a range of tools and components such as Canvas, Image, Text, Button, and Slider. These components can be combined and customized to create complex UI systems that respond to player input in real-time.

Overall, the UI is a critical component of any mobile game developed with Unity, and careful attention should be paid to its design and usability to ensure an enjoyable and engaging player experience. By using Unity's UI system and following best practices in UI design, beginners can create compelling and intuitive UIs for their mobile games.

Creating user interfaces in Unity

Creating user interfaces in Unity is an essential aspect of mobile game development. It is the graphical representation of the game's functionality, and it is what the player interacts with. The user interface (UI) is responsible for displaying important information such as the player's score, health, and other game components.

Unity provides a variety of tools to create user interfaces easily. The UI system is designed to be flexible, allowing developers to create complex and dynamic interfaces. The system includes a range of UI elements such as buttons, text fields, and sliders that can be customized to fit the game's theme and style.

To create a user interface in Unity, the first thing to do is to add a canvas to the scene. The canvas is the root element for all UI elements in the scene. It is responsible for rendering the UI elements and managing their hierarchy. Once the canvas is added, developers can begin to add UI elements to it.

Unity provides a range of UI elements that can be used to create different types of interfaces. For example, buttons can be used to create clickable elements that trigger actions, while sliders can be used to adjust values such as volume or brightness. Text fields can be used to display information such as the player's score, health, or other game components.

One of the most significant advantages of Unity's UI system is the ability to create dynamic interfaces. Developers can create interfaces that change based on the player's actions or game events. This can keep the player engaged and provide a more immersive experience.

To create dynamic interfaces, Unity provides various scripting options. Developers can use C# scripts to manipulate UI elements based on game events or player inputs. For example, developers can create a button that changes color when the player hovers over it.

In conclusion, creating user interfaces in Unity is an essential aspect of mobile game development. Unity's UI system provides a flexible and powerful set of tools that make it easy for developers to create complex and dynamic interfaces. With a little bit of practice, anyone can create beautiful and engaging user interfaces for their mobile games.

Adding buttons and text

In mobile game development, adding buttons and text is an essential part of creating an engaging and interactive game. Buttons are used to allow players to navigate through the game, make choices, and interact with the game's elements. Text, on the other hand, is used to provide information, instructions, and feedback to the player.

Adding Buttons

Unity provides a variety of tools for creating buttons, and the process is straightforward. First, you need to create a canvas, which serves as the root object for all UI elements. Then, you can add a button component to any game object, such as an image or a panel, and customize its appearance by setting its properties.

To create a button, you can use the Unity Editor or write a script. The Editor provides a visual interface for designing buttons, while scripting allows you to create more complex behavior, such as changing the button's appearance or triggering events.

Adding Text

Text is an essential part of any game, as it provides information and feedback to the player. Unity's UI system provides several options for adding text, such as text components, labels, and text meshes.

To add text, you need to create a text component and set its properties, such as font, size, color, and alignment. You can also use rich text formatting, such as bold, italic, underline, and color tags, to create more visually appealing text.

Conclusion

Adding buttons and text is a crucial part of mobile game development, as it allows players to interact with the game and provides essential information and feedback. Unity's UI system provides a range of tools for creating buttons and text, and with a little practice, you can create engaging and intuitive interfaces for your games.

Creating menus and screens

Menus and screens are an essential part of any game, as they allow players to navigate through the game and access various features. In Unity, you can create menus and screens using the GUI (Graphical User Interface) system, which provides a user-friendly interface for designing and implementing menus and screens.

To create a menu or screen in Unity, you will first need to create a Canvas object, which serves as the container for all the GUI elements. You can create a Canvas object by selecting "GameObject" from the menu bar, choosing "UI," and then selecting "Canvas." Once you have a Canvas object, you can add GUI elements to it, such as buttons, text fields, and images.

To add a button to your menu or screen, select the Canvas object in the Hierarchy window, and then click on the "Create" button in the Inspector window. Choose "UI" and then "Button" from the drop-down menu. You can then customize the button's appearance and functionality by adjusting its properties in the Inspector window.

To add a text field to your menu or screen, follow the same steps as adding a button, but choose "Input Field" instead. You can then customize the text field's appearance and functionality by adjusting its properties in the Inspector window.

To add an image to your menu or screen, select the Canvas object in the Hierarchy window, and then click on the "Create" button in the Inspector window. Choose "UI" and then "Image" from the drop-down menu. You can then customize the image's appearance by choosing an image file and adjusting its properties in the Inspector window.

In addition to creating menus and screens, you can also create transitions between them. For example, you might create a menu that leads to a settings screen, or a game over screen that leads to a main menu. To create a transition, you will need to use Unity's scripting system to define the logic for when and how the transition occurs.

In summary, creating menus and screens is an essential part of mobile game development with Unity. By using the GUI system and Unity's scripting system, you can create user-friendly interfaces that allow players to navigate through your game and access various features. With a little practice, you can create menus and screens that are both functional and visually appealing, helping to enhance the overall player experience.

Physics

What is physics?

Physics is the study of matter, energy, and the interactions between them. It is a fundamental branch of science that seeks to explain how the universe works at the most basic level. In the context of game development, physics is an essential part of creating realistic and engaging gameplay.

Physics in Unity

In Unity, physics is handled by the physics engine, which is a set of algorithms that simulate the laws of physics in a virtual environment. This enables objects in the game to interact with each other in a way that is consistent with the real world. For example, if a ball is thrown at a wall, it will bounce off the wall in a realistic manner, based on factors such as the angle of impact and the elasticity of the ball.

Physics Components in Unity

Unity provides a number of physics components that can be used to add physics to game objects. These include:

- Rigidbody: This component simulates the physical properties of an object, such as mass, velocity, and gravity.

- Collider: This component defines the shape of an object and determines how it interacts with other objects in the game.

- Joint: This component allows objects to be connected together, such as a rope connecting two objects.

- Physics Material: This component defines the physical properties of a surface, such as its friction and bounciness.

Using these components, game developers can create a wide variety of gameplay mechanics that are based on physics. For example, a game might feature a puzzle where the player must use objects with different physical properties to solve the puzzle. Or, a game might feature a platformer where the player must jump and navigate through a world that is filled with physics-based obstacles.

Conclusion

In summary, physics is a fundamental part of game development, and Unity provides a powerful set of tools for creating realistic and engaging physics-based gameplay. By using the physics components and algorithms provided by Unity, game developers can create a wide variety of gameplay mechanics that are based on the laws of physics. Whether you are a beginner or an experienced game developer, understanding the basics of physics is essential for creating successful mobile games in Unity.

Adding physics to game objects

Unity is a powerful game engine that provides developers with a wide range of tools to create engaging games. One of the key features that make Unity stand out is its physics engine. By adding physics to game objects, developers can create realistic and immersive gaming experiences that are sure to captivate players. In this subchapter, we will explore how to add physics to game objects in Unity.

The first step in adding physics to game objects is to create a physics-based game object. To do this, select the game object from the hierarchy and click on the Add Component button. From the dropdown menu, select Physics and choose the appropriate physics component for your game object. For example, if you want your game object to have gravity, you can add a Rigidbody component.

Once you have added physics to your game object, you can start tweaking its properties in the Inspector window. You can adjust the mass, drag, and angular drag properties to control how the game object moves and interacts with other objects in the game world.

Another important aspect of adding physics to game objects is colliders. Colliders are used to define the shape of the game object and how it interacts with other objects in the game world. To add a collider, select the game object and click on the Add Component button. From the dropdown menu, select Physics and choose the appropriate collider component for your game object.

In addition to colliders, Unity also provides developers with a range of physics materials that can be used to simulate different types of surfaces. For example, you can use a bouncy material to create a trampoline or a slippery material to create an ice rink.

By adding physics to game objects, developers can create dynamic and immersive gaming experiences that are sure to keep players engaged. Whether you are creating a mobile game or a PC game, Unity's physics engine provides you with the tools you need to bring your game world to life.

Understanding colliders and rigidbodies

When it comes to creating games in Unity, understanding colliders and rigidbodies is crucial. Colliders are components that define the shape of an object in the game world, while rigidbodies are components that determine how an object moves and interacts with other objects.

Colliders come in various shapes, such as boxes, spheres, and capsules, and are used to detect collisions with other objects in the game. When two colliders intersect, a collision event is triggered, allowing you to perform actions such as playing a sound, spawning particles, or applying damage to the objects.

Rigidbodies, on the other hand, are used to simulate physics in the game world. They allow objects to move and interact with each other based on physical laws such as gravity, friction, and velocity. You can add forces or torque to a rigidbody to make it move, and you can also apply constraints to restrict its movement in certain directions.

To create a collider or rigidbody, simply add the corresponding component to your object in the Unity editor. You can then adjust the properties of the component to customize its behavior. For example, you can set the mass and drag of a rigidbody to control its movement, or you can set the size and shape of a collider to match the object's appearance.

It's important to note that adding too many colliders or rigidbodies to your game can cause performance issues, so it's best to use them only when necessary. You can also optimize your game by using simpler collider shapes, such as boxes instead of spheres, and by disabling rigidbody physics on objects that don't need it.

In summary, understanding colliders and rigidbodies is essential for creating games in Unity. By using these components effectively, you can create realistic physics simulations and engaging gameplay mechanics that will keep your players coming back for more.

Applying forces and gravity

In order to create engaging and immersive mobile games in Unity, it is important to understand the principles of applying forces and gravity to game objects. These principles are crucial in creating realistic physics and movements in a game, and can greatly enhance the overall user experience.

When applying forces to game objects, it is important to understand that these forces can be applied in various directions and magnitudes. For example, you can apply a force to an object to make it move forward, or apply a force to an object to make it jump. These forces can be controlled through scripts and can be adjusted based on various game events and interactions.

Gravity is another important principle to consider when developing mobile games in Unity. Gravity is a force that pulls objects towards each other, and is a fundamental principle in creating realistic physics in games. In Unity, gravity can be applied to game objects through the use of physics components, such as a Rigidbody or a Collider.

One important aspect to consider when applying forces and gravity to game objects is the use of mass. Mass is a property of an object that determines its resistance to movement and its ability to be affected by external forces. In Unity, the mass of an object can be adjusted through the use of a Rigidbody component, and can greatly affect the way that object moves and interacts with other game objects.

Overall, understanding the principles of applying forces and gravity is crucial in creating engaging and realistic mobile games in Unity. By understanding how to apply these principles to game objects, developers can create more immersive and interactive games that will keep players engaged for longer periods of time.

Animation

What is animation?

Animation is a vital aspect of game development, and without it, games would be lifeless and flat. In simple terms, animation is the process of bringing static images to life by adding movement and sound. In game development, animation is used to create characters, objects, and environments that move and interact with the player.

Animation can be achieved using various techniques such as traditional hand-drawn animation, stop-motion animation, or computer-generated animation. However, in modern game development, most animations are created using software tools such as Unity. Unity is an incredibly powerful game development engine that provides users with a range of tools to create animations for their games.

Animations in Unity are created using a combination of keyframes and animation curves. Keyframes are points in time that define the starting and ending positions of an object or character. Animation curves, on the other hand, are used to define how an object moves between keyframes. Unity provides users with a range of animation curves that can be used to create smooth and fluid animations.

One of the most important aspects of animation is timing. Timing is critical when creating animations, as it determines how objects move and interact with each other. A poorly timed animation can ruin the overall experience of a game, whereas a well-timed animation can enhance the player's experience and make the game more enjoyable.

In conclusion, animation is a critical aspect of game development, and as a beginner, it's important to learn the basics of animation to create engaging and exciting games. With the right tools and techniques, anyone can create stunning animations that bring their games to life. Unity provides users with a range of tools to create animations, and with practice, anyone can become a master animator.

Creating animations in Unity

Creating animations in Unity is an essential aspect of game development. Animations bring your game characters and objects to life by adding movement and visual effects. Unity has a powerful animation system that allows you to create complex animations easily. In this subchapter, we will guide you through the process of creating animations in Unity.

The first step in creating animations in Unity is to import your 3D models into the game engine. Unity supports a wide range of 3D modelling software such as Blender, Maya, and 3DS Max. Once imported, you can start creating animations using Unity's animation system.

The animation system in Unity is based on the concept of animation clips. An animation clip is a set of keyframes that define the position, rotation, and scale of your game objects over time. You can create animation clips by using the Animation window in Unity.

To create an animation clip, select the object you want to animate in the Scene view, and then open the Animation window by selecting Window > Animation. In the Animation window, you can create keyframes by selecting the object's transform properties and setting their values at different points in time. Unity will automatically interpolate the values between keyframes, creating smooth animations.

Unity also supports the creation of complex animations using the Animator controller. The Animator controller is a tool that allows you to create state machines that control the flow of your game's animations. You can use the Animator controller to create animations that respond to user input or game events.

In conclusion, creating animations in Unity is an essential skill for mobile game developers. With Unity's powerful animation system, you can bring your game characters and objects to life, adding movement and visual effects that enhance the player experience. By following the steps outlined in this subchapter, you can create complex animations easily and take your mobile game development to the next level.

Adding animations to game objects

Adding Animations to Game Objects

Animations are essential in any game. They bring life to characters and objects, making them more engaging and interesting to interact with. In Unity, adding animations to game objects is a straightforward process that beginners can quickly learn.

To add an animation, you first need to create an animation clip. Animation clips are assets that store animation data. To create an animation clip, select the game object you want to animate in the Hierarchy window and click the "Create" button in the Animation window. Alternatively, you can right-click the game object and choose "Create Animation" from the context menu.

Once you have created an animation clip, you can start adding animation keyframes. Keyframes are positions in time where you define how the game object should look and behave. To add a keyframe, move the game object to the desired position and click the "Add Keyframe" button in the Animation window.

You can also modify the animation curve to adjust the timing and intensity of the animation. The curve editor allows you to create smooth transitions between keyframes and add more complexity to your animations.

After creating the animation clip, you need to add it to the game object's animator controller. The animator controller is responsible for managing all the animations for a specific game object. To add the animation clip, drag and drop it into the animator controller window.

Finally, you need to trigger the animation in your game. You can do this by using an animator component or a script. The animator component allows you to play, pause, and stop the animation based on specific events. Alternatively, you can use a script to control the animation's behavior and timing.

In conclusion, adding animations to game objects is an essential skill for any mobile game developer using Unity. By following the steps outlined above, you can quickly create engaging and dynamic animations that will enhance your game's overall experience. Remember to experiment with different animation curves and keyframes to create unique and exciting animations.

Animating user interfaces

Animating User Interfaces

User Interfaces are a key component of any game, especially mobile games, as they provide players with the necessary information to navigate through the game. Animating User Interfaces adds an extra layer of engagement to the game, making it more immersive and enjoyable for players. In this subchapter, we will explore the basics of animating user interfaces in Unity.

Creating Animations

Animations in Unity can be created using the Animation window, which can be accessed by clicking on Window > Animation. The Animation window allows you to create and edit animations for any component in your game, including User Interfaces. To create an animation, select the component you want to animate and click on the "Create" button in the Animation window. This will create a new animation clip that can be edited and played back.

Animating User Interfaces

Animating User Interfaces in Unity is similar to animating any other component in the game. You can animate things like text, images, buttons, and even entire panels using the Animation window. To animate a UI element, you need to add the component you want to animate to the Animation window as a property. Once added, you can create keyframes and adjust the properties of the component over time to create the desired animation.

Types of Animations

There are several types of animations that can be used to animate User Interfaces in Unity, including:

Fade In/Out: This animation is used to make the UI element gradually appear or disappear on the screen.

Scale: This animation is used to make the UI element grow or shrink in size.

Move: This animation is used to make the UI element move from one position to another on the screen.

Rotate: This animation is used to make the UI element rotate around its center point.

Conclusion

Animating User Interfaces in Unity is a great way to make your game more engaging and immersive. With the Animation window, you can create a variety of animations to bring your UI to life. By using the different types of animations available in Unity, you can create unique and dynamic UI elements that will keep players coming back for more.

Sound and Music

Adding sound effects to games

Adding sound effects to games is an essential aspect of game development that plays a crucial role in enhancing the overall gameplay experience. Sound effects can create a sense of immersion, evoke emotions, and add an extra layer of excitement to the game. In this subchapter, we will explore the process of adding sound effects to games using Unity, a popular game development engine.

The first step in adding sound effects to your game is to create or acquire the audio files that you want to use. You can either create your sound effects using a digital audio workstation (DAW) or download them from websites that offer royalty-free audio files. Once you have your audio files, you can import them into Unity by simply dragging and dropping them into the Assets folder.

After importing your audio files, you can start adding them to your game objects. In Unity, you can add audio sources to game objects, which emit sound when triggered by certain events. For example, you can add a gunshot sound effect to a gun object and set it to play when the player shoots.

You can also add ambient sound effects to your game by creating an audio source that plays continuously in the background. This can create a sense of realism and immersion in your game, especially for games that take place in outdoor environments.

Unity also offers a range of tools and features for modifying and enhancing your sound effects. For example, you can adjust the volume, pitch, and spatialization of your audio sources to create a more dynamic and immersive soundscape. You can also use audio effects such as reverb, echo, and distortion to add depth and texture to your sound effects.

In conclusion, adding sound effects to your game is a crucial aspect of game development that can greatly enhance the overall gameplay experience. With Unity, you can easily add and modify sound effects to create a more immersive and exciting game.

Creating background music

Background music is an essential part of any mobile game, and it helps to enhance the overall gameplay experience. It sets the tone and mood of the game, and it can help to drive the emotions of the player. Creating background music for your mobile game is an exciting process, and it requires a bit of creativity and technical know-how. In this subchapter, we'll take a look at some tips and tricks for creating background music for your mobile game.

1. Determine the mood and tone of your game

Before you start creating the background music, you need to determine the mood and tone of your game. Is it a fast-paced action game, or is it a relaxing puzzle game? The music should match the tone of your game, and it should help to enhance the player's experience.

2. Choose the right instruments

Once you have determined the tone and mood of your game, you need to choose the right instruments for your background music. For example, if you're creating a game with a medieval theme, you might want to use instruments like the lute, harp, or flute to create a more authentic feel.

3. Create a loopable track

Background music in games needs to be loopable, meaning that it can be played on a loop without sounding repetitive. When creating your music, keep this in mind and make sure that the different sections of your track flow seamlessly into each other.

4. Use sound effects sparingly

While sound effects can add to the overall experience of your game, they can also be distracting if overused. Use sound effects sparingly and make sure that they complement the background music rather than compete with it.

5. Test your music in-game

Once you have created your background music, test it in your game to see how it sounds in context. Make any necessary adjustments to ensure that the music fits well with the gameplay and enhances the player's overall experience.

Creating background music for your mobile game is an exciting process, and with these tips and tricks, you can create music that enhances the player's experience and sets the tone and mood of your game.

Using audio sources in Unity

Using audio sources in Unity

Audio is an essential element in any mobile game development project. It helps to create a more immersive and engaging experience for players. Unity provides different audio sources that can be used to create sound effects, background music, and other audio elements for your game.

In this section, we will discuss the different audio sources available in Unity and how to use them effectively in your game.

Audio Sources in Unity

Unity provides different audio sources that can be used to create different audio effects in your game. These audio sources include:

1. Audio Listener: This audio source is used to capture audio from the game environment and plays it through the speakers or headphones of the player's device.

2. Audio Source: This audio source is used to play audio clips in the game. You can use it to create sound effects or play background music.

3. Audio Reverb Zone: This audio source is used to create reverb effects in the game environment. It can be used to simulate different environments such as a cave, a concert hall, or an open space.

Using Audio Sources in Unity

To use audio sources in your Unity project, you need to follow these steps:

1. Import Audio Clips: You can import audio clips into your Unity project by dragging and dropping them into the project window. You can also use the Import button in the project window to import audio files.

2. Create Audio Sources: To create an audio source, you need to add an Audio Source component to a game object in your scene. You can do this by selecting the game object and then clicking on the Add Component button in the Inspector window. From the menu, select Audio > Audio Source.

3. Configure Audio Sources: You can configure the properties of your audio sources to create different audio effects. For example, you can adjust the volume, pitch, and loop properties of your audio sources to create sound effects or background music.

4. Add Audio Sources to Game Objects: You can add audio sources to different game objects in your scene to create different audio effects. For example, you can add an audio source to a character in your game to create sound effects for their movements.

Conclusion

Using audio sources in Unity is essential for creating immersive and engaging mobile games. With the different audio sources available in Unity, you can create sound effects, background music, and other audio elements for your game. By following the steps outlined in this section, you can effectively use audio sources in your Unity project to create a more immersive and engaging game experience for your players.

Building and Exporting

Building your game

Building your game is the ultimate goal of game development. It's where all the hard work and planning come into play. In this subchapter, we will look at the different stages involved in building a game using Unity. Unity is a powerful game engine that allows you to create stunning games for mobile devices. With its intuitive interface and easy-to-use tools, you can quickly develop your game and make it ready for release.

The first step in building your game is to plan it out. You need to have a clear idea of what your game will be about, what kind of gameplay it will have, and what features it will include. This will help you to create a solid foundation for your game and ensure that it meets the expectations of your target audience.

Once you have a plan, you can start creating the game's assets. This includes everything from the game's graphics and sound effects to its level design and character animations. Unity comes with a range of tools that make it easy to create these assets, so even if you have no prior experience in game development, you can still create high-quality assets for your game.

Next, you need to start putting everything together. This involves creating the game's scenes and levels, adding in the assets you created, and programming the game's mechanics. Unity's visual scripting system, called UnityScript, makes it easy to create complex gameplay mechanics without having to write any code.

Finally, you need to test your game thoroughly to ensure that it's bug-free and ready for release. This involves playing through the game multiple times, identifying any issues, and fixing them before releasing the game to the public. Unity comes with a range of testing tools that make it easy to test your game on different devices and platforms, ensuring that it runs smoothly on all of them.

In conclusion, building a game using Unity is a fun and rewarding experience, even for beginners. With its intuitive interface and easy-to-use tools, you can quickly create high-quality games for mobile devices. By following the steps outlined in this subchapter, you can create your own mobile game and share it with the world.

Exporting your game for mobile devices

Exporting your game for mobile devices is an essential step in the game development process. With Unity, you can export your game to different platforms, including iOS and Android. In this subchapter, we will guide you through the process of exporting your game for mobile devices.

Before exporting your game, you need to make sure that it is optimized for mobile devices. This includes optimizing the graphics, audio, and gameplay for mobile devices. Mobile devices have limited resources, and you need to ensure that your game runs smoothly on different devices.

Once your game is optimized for mobile devices, you can export it for iOS and Android. To export your game for iOS, you need to have a Mac with Xcode installed. Xcode is the development environment for iOS, and it is essential for exporting your game to iOS. You also need to have an Apple Developer account to publish your game on the App Store.

To export your game for Android, you need to have Android Studio installed. Android Studio is the development environment for Android, and it is essential for exporting your game to Android. You also need to have a Google Play Developer account to publish your game on the Google Play Store.

When exporting your game for mobile devices, you need to ensure that it meets the requirements of each platform. Each platform has its own set of requirements, and you need to follow them to ensure that your game is accepted on the app store.

In conclusion, exporting your game for mobile devices is an essential step in the game development process. With Unity, you can export your game to different platforms, including iOS and Android. You need to ensure that your game is optimized for mobile devices and meets the requirements of each platform. By following these steps, you can publish your game on the app store and reach a wider audience.

Testing your game on different devices

Testing your game on different devices is a crucial step in mobile game development. It is important to ensure that your game runs smoothly on different devices and platforms to provide a seamless gaming experience to your players. Here are some tips for testing your game on different devices:

1. Use Unity Remote: Unity Remote is a handy tool that allows you to test your game on a mobile device without having to build and deploy it. You can connect your mobile device to your computer and use Unity Remote to test your game in real-time.

2. Test on different platforms: Your game should be tested on different platforms such as iOS and Android to ensure that it works on all devices. You can use emulators to test your game on different platforms.

3. Test on different screen sizes: It is important to test your game on different screen sizes to ensure that it is optimized for all devices. You can use the Unity Remote app to test your game on different screen sizes.

4. Test on low-end devices: It is important to test your game on low-end devices to ensure that it runs smoothly on all devices. You can use emulators or borrow low-end devices from friends or family to test your game.

5. Test for bugs and crashes: It is important to test your game for bugs and crashes to ensure that it provides a seamless gaming experience to your players. You can use debugging tools to find and fix bugs and crashes.

In conclusion, testing your game on different devices is an important step in mobile game development. It ensures that your game provides a seamless gaming experience to your players on all devices and platforms. Use the tips mentioned above to test your game and provide the best gaming experience to your players.

Conclusion

What have you learned?

The journey of game development can be an arduous one, especially for beginners. However, with Unity Game Development for Beginners, you have gained valuable knowledge and experience that will help you create exciting mobile games.

So, what have you learned? Firstly, you have learned how to use Unity, the most popular game engine, to develop mobile games. You have also learned how to use various tools, such as the Unity Editor, the Asset Store, and the scripting language C#.

You have learned how to create 2D and 3D games, design game levels, and use physics and animations to create realistic movements and interactions. You have also learned how to add audio, graphics, and UI elements to your games, making them more engaging and interactive.

In addition, you have learned how to design games that are optimized for mobile devices, including how to use touch and gesture controls, and how to optimize game performance for mobile devices.

Moreover, you have learned how to publish your games on various app stores, including Apple App Store and Google Play Store, and how to monetize your games through in-app purchases and ads.

Perhaps most importantly, you have learned how to think like a game developer and how to approach game development with a problem-solving mindset. You have learned how to break down complex tasks into smaller, more manageable steps, and how to test and debug your games to ensure that they are of high quality and error-free.

In conclusion, Unity Game Development for Beginners has taught you a lot about mobile game development with Unity. With this knowledge and experience, you are well on your way to creating exciting and engaging mobile games that people will love to play. Keep learning, experimenting, and creating, and who knows, you might just create the next big hit game!

What's next?

Congratulations! You have completed this step-by-step guide to creating mobile games with Unity. By now, you should have a good understanding of the basics of game development and how to use Unity to create your own games.

So, what's next? Well, the world of game development is constantly evolving, and there is always more to learn. Here are a few suggestions for what you can do next:

1. Keep practicing: The more you practice, the better you will get. Experiment with different types of games and try to create something that is unique and fun. Don't be afraid to make mistakes — that's how you learn!

2. Learn more about Unity: While this guide has covered the basics of Unity, there is still a lot more to learn. Check out Unity's official website for tutorials, documentation, and forums where you can ask questions and get help from other developers.

3. Join a community: There are many online communities for game developers, such as Reddit's /r/gamedev and the Unity Forums. Joining a community can help you meet other developers, get feedback on your games, and stay up-to-date on the latest trends and technologies.

4. Publish your game: Once you have created a game that you are proud of, consider publishing it to the app store. This can be a great way to get feedback from real users and potentially make some money from your game.

5. Keep learning: Game development is a constantly evolving field, and there is always something new to learn. Keep reading blogs, watching tutorials, and experimenting with new tools and technologies to stay ahead of the curve.

In conclusion, creating mobile games with Unity can be a fun and rewarding experience. By following this guide and continuing to learn and practice, you can create your own amazing games that people will love to play. Good luck and happy game development!

Final thoughts.

Final thoughts

Congratulations on making it to the end of Unity Game Development for Beginners! You are now equipped with the necessary skills and knowledge to create your very own mobile games using Unity.

As you embark on your game development journey, remember that the learning process never ends. There will always be new features and updates to Unity, and it's important to stay up-to-date on these changes to keep your games fresh and relevant.

In addition to keeping up with the latest updates, it's important to continue practicing and experimenting with different game mechanics and designs. The more you practice, the better you will become at creating engaging and entertaining games.

When it comes to mobile game development with Unity, there are a few key things to keep in mind. First, it's important to optimize your game for mobile devices, taking into account factors such as screen size, resolution, and performance. Second, consider incorporating features such as in-app purchases and ads to monetize your game.

Finally, don't forget to have fun! Game development can be a challenging and rewarding experience, but it's important to enjoy the process and not get too bogged down in perfectionism. Remember that mistakes and failures are a natural part of the learning process, and can often lead to even better ideas and solutions.

Thank you for choosing Unity Game Development for Beginners as your guide to mobile game development with Unity. We hope that this book has been helpful in getting you started on your game development journey, and we can't wait to see the amazing games you create!

www.ingramcontent.com/pod-product-compliance
Lightning Source LLC
LaVergne TN
LVHW051743050326
832903LV00029B/2694